Looking for Patterns

By M.C. Hall

Scott Foresman
is an imprint of

PEARSON

Glenview, Illinois • Boston, Massachusetts • Chandler, Arizona •
Upper Saddle River, New Jersey

Photographs

Every effort has been made to secure permission and provide appropriate credit for photographic material. The publisher deeply regrets any omission and pledges to correct errors called to its attention in subsequent editions.

Unless otherwise acknowledged, all photographs are the property of Pearson Education, Inc.

Photo locators denoted as follows: Top (T), Center (C), Bottom (B), Left (L), Right (R), Background (Bkgd)

Opener: ©Melba Photo Agency/Alamy
1 Karl Shone/©DK Images
3 Brian Cosgrove/©DK Images
4 ©Melba Photo Agency/Alamy
5 ©Robert Gruber/PhotoLibrary Group, Ltd.
6 Geoff Dann/©DK Images
7 Jupiter Images
8 Jupiter Images
9 Jupiter Images
10 ©Elisabeth Coelfen/SuperStock
11 Karl Shone/©DK Images
12 Tim Ridley/©DK Images

ISBN 13: 978-0-328-46909-3
ISBN 10:   0-328-46909-2

Clouds have different shapes and sizes. They make patterns.

Other patterns in nature help us understand our world.

You can find patterns on the ground. These sand dunes show us which way the wind was blowing.

Animal tracks make patterns. These tracks tell us that this animal has webbed feet.

The patterns of flower petals help us tell flowers apart. This flower is a buttercup.

The pattern of this web tells us what kind of spider made it.

The sun makes a pattern in the sky. It seems to move across the sky from east to west. The sun's pattern helps us tell time.

The moon's shape seems to change a little each day. This pattern tells us that the moon moves around Earth.

Some animals have fur with patterns such as spots or stripes. The pattern on this deer tells us it's a baby.

Different trees have leaves with different shapes. This maple leaf has a pattern of five main points.

The lines and ridges on these shells form another of nature's patterns. Look for more of nature's patterns wherever you go!